Phenomenology of the Feral

Julia Rose Lewis

NEWTON-LE-WILLOWS

Published in the United Kingdom in 2018
by The Knives Forks And Spoons Press,
51 Pipit Avenue,
Newton-le-Willows,
Merseyside,
WA12 9RG.

ISBN 978-1-912211-08-1

Copyright © Julia Rose Lewis, 2018.

The right of Julia Rose Lewis to be identified as the author of this work has been asserted by her in accordance with the Copyrights, Designs and Patents act of 1988. All rights reserved. No part of this publication may be reproduced, stored in a retrieval system, transmitted in any form or by any means, electronic, photocopying, recording or otherwise, without prior permission of the publisher.

Acknowledgments:

Poems from this collection have been published by: *Atrocity*, *The Gambler Mag*, *Poetry Wales*, *Enchanting Verses*, *The Learned Pig*, *3am Magazine*, *The Missing Slate*, *Glint Literary Journal*, *Dead King Magazine*, *Losslit*, and in *Rasputin: a Poetry Thread*. 'Zeroing Event' was published in pamphlet form by Zarf Editions.

The cover image is *Bunticles* by Phineas X. Jones (http://octophant.us)

For Paul Grobstein

Table of Contents

Zeroing Event
So Just Fault	11
We, Our Perishable Food	12
Wobbles!	13
Something wilder than Iowa	14
Butter the Child of the Corn and Trees Not Found in Iowa	15
Too White to Photograph	16
Ihadafriend	17
4/11/15	18
The whole movement is executed without a pause	19
My favorite word that rhymes with warm	20
Thanksgiving	21
If Number, Then Name	22
Zeroing Event	23
Corner of Your Eye	24
Definition of Madness	25
Fundamental Theorem of Christmas	26
Staring at the Sun	27
Does Radiation	29

Phenomenology of the Feral
The Rottweiler's Guide to the Dog Owner	33
Phenomenology of the Feral I	34
Phenomenology of the Feral II	35
Phenomenology of the Feral III	36
The Assembly of the Head	37
Phenomenology of the Feral IV	38

Phenomenology of the Feral V	39
Phenomenology of the Feral VI	40
Phenomenology of the Feral VII	41
Phenomenology of the Feral VIII	42
Cognitive Unconscious I	43
Phenomenology of the Feral IX	44
Oryctolagus Cuniculus	45
Phenomenology of the Feral X	46
Phenomenology of the Feral XI	47
Phenomenology of the Feral XII	48
Phenomenology of the Feral XIII	49
Phenomenology of the Feral XIV	50
Cognitive Unconscious II	51
Gilfaethwy	52
When in Doubt, Throw Grobstein on the Table	53
Maid of Refrigerators	55
Merely	56

Breathing Underwater

Breathing Underwater I	59
Breathing Underwater II	60
Breathing Underwater III	61
Breathing Underwater IV	62
Breathing Underwater V	63
Admiration of Hermit Crabs	64
Breathing Underwater VI	65
Breathing Underwater VII	66
Breathing Underwater VIII	67
Breathing Underwater IX	68
Breathing Underwater X	69
Breathing Underwater XI	70
Breathing Underwater XII	71
Breathing Underwater XIII	72
Breathing Underwater XIV	73
Breathing Underwater XV	74
Emissary	75
Breathing Underwater XVI	77

Summer of Gummy Bears

Lingering Question	81
I Bring You Bears and Raspberries	82
The Greening of the Bears	83
Ginger Bears with the Wifey	84
The Quaker Kind	85
"This is vintage Julia"	86
Cherries to Old Nantucket	87
Sand Woman, Sour Woman	88
Hair of the Gummy Bear	89
Happy Stroll	90

Notes — 91
Acknowledgements — 92

Zeroing Event

So Just Fault

Out of the pewter, I handed over my bottle of pills.
Longing is pyriform.
Eyes light blue, no grey, but the lines appeared clearly like the winter coat for horses are cold.
Please sing again putting on our coats: chaos, cognitive unconscious, compost pile.
Depression surprises with boredom the long hours of orange light.
Tell me what you would say about transparency versus opacity in therapy and poetry and butter.
You age gain, the paring knife is beautiful.
Food being the opposite of sex if you say so, then the recipe.
There is hot narrative here.
Purr with hair like my eleventh grade english teacher.
I want to feed you a pear, slice by slice, you see a peer really?

Julia Rose Lewis

We, Our Perishable Food

The first summer I lived in Iowa it was so hot I fantasized about climbing into the refrigerator.

So much corn dried up and died. Two years later, I was listening to a radio station in Indiana called Korn! It was the first time I had ever heard someone with a New Zealand accent sing along to country music. When we got off the highway for dinner, our waitress confused vegetarian with lesbian. We counted water towers on the drive back to Iowa City. If you put a physicist and a biologist in a car together for nine hours, then they will find something to quantify. For the first time, I'm not summering in the midwest. Now does not one sick hen sound like one second? Book alive like a bird, they had to kill five million chickens on a farm in north western Iowa because of bird flu. These hens are little more than one percent of the nation's egg layers, yet there may be consequences, the Iowa Poultry Association Executive Director said. Which came first the chicken or the egg?

Which came first the ribosome or the protein?

Phenomenology of the Feral

Wobbles!

Which came first: the ribosome or the protein?
Oh wow ribonucleoprotein now.
Biological definition of life is the lie of the molecule, the RNA world hypothesis.
Base all ways, small subunit is the reader;
Large subunit is the joiner.
Experiments all: store your RNA as DNA as it is more stable. Before
Searches

!

Julia Rose Lewis

Something Wilder than Iowa

                      Would be a tall experiment.   You are on a pear.
We, our perishable food, refrigerators white, like eggshells protect.   After the ford model T was introduced, refrigerators cost more than cars for many years.   On machines and pollution, think of the air, think of the increasing concentration of carbon monoxide before the two-way catalytic converters created carbon dioxide.   A refrigerator is not a Faraday cage, but a microwave is.   Physical chemists accidentally melted chocolate bars with microwaves in the laboratory.   Books taste like chicken: bone white, fat light, muscle is surprising me.   To sing the incubator more effective for bacterial growth, because those plasmids slow them down.   The rhyme, the White was laboratory and mentor, and the white refrigerator.   The experiment time, I'm not falling and fully grown yet planning.   Please said.

Butter the Child of the Corn and Trees Not Found in Iowa

Third time's a charm, a day old corn muffin, a savings of fifty percent.
Southern corn muffins are savoury and ivory
Northern corn muffins are now, sweet and honey.

The sun and the blank page only egg-like. My eyes are toasted corn muffin brown;
his eyes are not cornflower blue.
White plastic teeth frown at the extra butter nose.

Why did my friend hide my travel mug in the refrigerator?

Julia Rose Lewis

Too White to Photograph

An orgasm is like a refrigerator found on the side of the road,
the water on white blinds.

This is my refraction,
my change in direction of propagation a wave.

I am due to change its medium of transmission.
My sport utility vehicle has a continuously variable transmission.

Mean then while the rain colours,
dark things should just be black and not blue.

> Kind of you to conserve the energy
> to conserve the momentum kneeling.

To bind, the ribonucleic acid forms a kink-turn motif. Recognition is thus biting.
This is reflection: Susan White,

"our goal is to understand how some of these irregular structural features contribute to the thermodynamic stability of the RNA molecule and function as sites for protein recognition."[1]

Ihadafriend

What is the wildest thing you could do?
Idha said. Have you read my
Letters yet? She said. Are you ok?

Dear rest, and the three cats sank.
Emu who is my muse? What about rolling my Rs?
Six ticks, I cease to practice.

The seventh thing is not given.

4/11/15

"I only know when he
began to dance with me.

I could have danced, danced, danced all night!"[2]
Bryn Mawr time is plus ten minutes;

London time is plus half an hour.
After the sweat dried,

thank you points to
boxing as counterintuitive as quantum mechanics.

So strike the slippery brain
sweet on science.

On cinders and ballet slippers, really my fair lady,
Apollo's Lady.

Pumpkins, mice, and pear cider remain
after a single baby elephant stampedes about London.

The Whole Movement is Executed Without a Pause

Jeté en tournant:

fifth position, right foot front
slip into the soft and loud
execute a *sissonne tombée* to the
music swelling my involuntary nervous system
fourth position *croisée* into a *demi-plié* on the right foot,

bending the body forward,
from brain to science to sincere
coupé dessus left, throwing the right leg forward ninety degrees,
toward the refrigerator opposite of fright
making a quarter turn *en dehors*,

immediately spring into the air, continuing the turn to the right,
dwelling in my first time with a percussion instrument
and land on the right foot in *demi-plié*
excite
in *attitude croisé derriere*.

Julia Rose Lewis

My Favourite Word that Rhymes with Warm

Is tacoform.
Yellow corn, welsh rarebit, of course,

my ticket tells me the Spanish term for eating for taste,
not choreography.
Brace to let the safety out.

Before clasping with charm my six and a half inch wrist,
read the golden rabbit – he is cool and I am furry.

Thanksgiving

Ideal Reader,

Thank you for your generosity to me and chivalry towards my discussion. Between boxing and ballet lies dressage.

Your events have given me so many poems which I am afraid is like drinking from both sides of the coffee cup.

I love your fibonacci collaboration, the unfolding of Emily Galvin's poetry with greater breadth. Over and again I am struck by the curl of your fingers into a fist.

All the beast,

Julia and Lady

Julia Rose Lewis

If Number, Then Name

Begin alabamine, dakin, dorine (from longing), helvetium, anglohelvetium, astatine (unstable).

Down the metalloid diagonal, one under iodine the heaviest of halogens known to science, "the only interesting story in chemistry is reactions," Paul Grobstein said.
                      Astatine hydride is metal-like. Unlike the lighter halogens, it vaporizes so readily by means of radioactive heating, the goal is finding sufficient cooling for experimentation. This element has part of actium, neptunium, and uranium decay chains.
                      Dressage was performed, the first day (three-day event), meaning training.

Zeroing Event

Inside lead dating
grey thing for an ache to take
clay awaits body.

How many skin cells fall into a single piece of pottery? Be of four. It had to be bisque or biscuit fired before glaze fired. It had to face the potter's wheel, fortune ate it, throwing comes from twisting or turning. Of clay, the body can dance, from Carmina Burana, red skirt and circles of *tour jetés*. In earlier choreography it was greenware, it was leather-hard, it was bone-dry and fired. Fire is a property of orange not red gemstones.

How would you tell? A body of clay it must be kneaded and wedged to remove the elements air and water. That poetry is made of clay and hardened permanently by heat. It is ceramic-like a nonmetallic, non-melting solid.

Julia Rose Lewis

Corner of Your Eye

little men waiting,
little green men multiply
like rabbits – don't fight

All little green fluorescent rabbits come from the sea from *Aequorea victoria*. Albino rabbits are the result of artificial selection by human breeders. The protein of the green fluorescent jellyfish can be maintained through breeding. Alba, glows with a bright green light when illuminated with blue light. The body of the rabbit is clay waiting for an ache to take inside. Alive, a lighthouse, she is a chimerical

animal. Alien and lovable body is the example of the problem. Odo means unknown sample in the Bajoran language. Anomaly living with humanity. Roswell, time travel, Kemocite, what is known lies between changelings and gods. All the gods in this series are just other forms of life. Star Trek portrays science as curiosity, as a desire for the unknown, as a discussion.

This is deep space indeed.

Definition of Madness

Why is the loss the measure?
Of her black serendibite
fur, she is a three-
dimensional shadow.

Bring me a shadow in the
wintertime when shadows are
not hard to find. Her
long ears lost waste wait here. What
are shadows the measure of?

What is lost with the wasting
of time? I'm afraid
madness looks for a shadow.

Julia Rose Lewis

Fundamental Theorem of Christmas

Follow the rabbit,
the waxy black tattoo of
a brand on my thigh.

She is found: a spot of black that hops after the disappearing sun.
Day and darkness she follows the Apollo's Lady horse inside and outside.
Hopping after you staring at the sun.
A shadow, a daughter heliad, the first derivative of the sun's path through the sky.
Where the hair is thin, her ears are peach and skin in lightning.
Derivative of the sun with respect to time, she charges with the function.
She is the mud of time.
She is soft jet resulting from carbon compression and freshwater on the wood of a Monkey Puzzle – like tree.
This fossil is found in seams of shale, in air or under water.
It is the mourning stone.
Her dam was morning sun.
Her sire was Apollo.
Apollo's filly is the integral of the shadow.
The fundamental theorem of calculus states the differentiation and integration are each other's inverse.

Staring at the sun

I

the black spots they pirouette
about in tutus.

II

Photographic paper is
sensitive to blue.

III

The developer reduces;
the silver halide
gains an electron turning
into metallic
silver, the latent image.

IV

The silver halide
is never an astatide

V

The stop bath, stop time,
halves a minute; then fixer,
stop bath kills fixer.

Now fix her by dissolving
the light-sensitive
emulsion on the paper.
The second fixer
removes the undeveloped

and the water bath
removes the last chemicals.

Water was always
running over photographs,
tongs, and plastic tray.
A mortuary table
has ideal drainage.

The eight by tens hang above
the table dripping.

Epilogue

The white flash feels like
"all my charms are [over] thrown
and what strength I have's
my own which is most faint now
tis true I must be
here confined by you …"[3]

Does Radiation

The history of the crystalline material is told through its flaws. Natural crystalline materials hold impurity ions, stress dislocations, and other disturbances. These lead to humps and dips in the electric potential of the material. A dip in the electric field is a trap for an electron. Given enough energy these trapped electrons will escape; they will lose energy and emit photons. They are recovered by means of thermoluminescence made measurements.

Thermoluminescence is the dating of art if facts then zeroing event. To find the zeroing event, the total dose accumulated must be divided by the dose accumulating each year. The day my white rabbit died was the zeroing event. The opposite of lost is found.

Follow the rabbit
Alba art and science in
one body again.

The opposite of lost is joined together. Depression is a long unresolved conflict between the cognitive unconscious and the I-function. So that pottery is as close to depression as radioactive decay. Pear rent isotope to daughter isotope to granddaughter isotope. Patterns of inheritance named alpha decay, beta decay, positron emission electron capture, and isomeric transition. So repeats the high erratic pattern. Unstable as astatine, watch the half-lives fall away as radioactive decay in the time of the white rabbit. The opposite of lost is saved.

Phenomenology of the Feral

The Rottweiler's Guide to the Dog Owner
after S.J. Fowler

If you were a fruit,
what fruit would you be?
Black banana, fruit flies,
les ananas ne parlent pas,
(a little song of two children learning french on Canadian TV).

In middle school, the chair in the crypt.
The stack of cryptic poems high enough to use as a chair
& those who will never be sitting on it. Those who flower,
I flower you, you flower me golden, & Russian surrealism,
remember when I sledded into a tree in a yard without trees?

The black eye bloomed yellow. For the two who fold the chair
while your hair is wrapped in a towel; that counts as naked.
The talk, the Skype,
that neither of us remembers how to decline pooka
that was made of wood, & flowers.
And sea creatures, you only see the octopus
when I see the squid.

The diagnosis is a cup upside down a paradox.
That prozac in the hand held, not yet
sexual, but facing the wall with the fist
& not the street. Either fluoxetine is not treating this
or this is a side-effect. A paradox of sex, trust the bitch.
The two, like breasts, are two. Like kidneys, we need each other
and your head on my butt great & free, & outdoors
(you leave your boyfriend a note "do not forget to take her for a long walk").[4]

Julia Rose Lewis

Phenomenology of the Feral I
After the Meat Tree[5]

Man's best friend, woman's best friend are has a jay, and mere has an add. I flower mere and he follows me that was made of wood and flowers and see, it is pronounced mer as the french for sea not mere lie down you are drunk.   Remember the dog is not dead because you can not find its pulse; please go have sex with your fiancé now.

Phenomenology of the Feral II

How do we fit dogs,
flowers, hunters, and eagles
in the apartment?

Julia Rose Lewis

Phenomenology of the Feral III

She turned me on to wood dresses: the flowers of the oak, and the flowers of the broom, and the flowers of the meadowsweet, his midwestern speech. He hears it when I say water, my owner's Mid-Atlantic accent. It is too dark for him to see that hiraeth is tattooed on my left hind paw. In 'The Fourth Branch' of the *Mabinogion*,[6] we are sensitive to the earth's magnetic field as *canis lupus familiaris*.

The Assembly of the Head

Branwen,
begin and treat the root well

feed from fish and wild honey,
never hay collars and gate hammers.

One of three golden shoe makers,
the third branch is not given

of four branches of the *Mabinogion*.
Friendship of four and flour, a pair and a pregnant mouse,

five swine must breed to twice their number.
Ten may be able to save the white book from silver fish

book from brain from paper from tree from nervous stem
from the brain to behaviour is the hind end of the rabbit.

Seven men they buried Bran's head under the white hill
"Seven loads of baggage you see on these seven horses."

Julia Rose Lewis

Phenomenology of the Feral IV

The fans were the quieting part; I only heard him in my right ear. He wants to be the magician king, Math fab Mathonwy. If he had feet, not paws, then I would hold them arch to iliac crest. How faraway are his heels? The buck and doe escape from the hunting party once upon a time growing into the forest.

Phenomenology of the Feral V

metamorphosis
my claws catch on the grey cloth
of his shorts kneading

Julia Rose Lewis

Phenomenology of the Feral VI

Sweep the fallen plaster, wipe down the widow sill, the wall, and the moulding. Find the dustbin, and lift the trash bag. When the cinder dog returns from the dumpster, I shower him with the water shaken form my hair. He admires my failure to cook leeks in lieu of sleep, daffodils without the yell oh flowers. What about the rosa rugosa? What about the cat, the hunter of birds, the eagle at the meating tree?

Phenomenology of the Feral VII

the gutter and drains
raindrops were inside with us
lust, dust, must the mould

Julia Rose Lewis

Phenomenology of the Feral VIII

Be coming? Before sleeping in the fireplace, we do not notice the grey dust that might have been ashes. Life by leaf, the earliest tales can be found in the Red Book of Hergest and the White Book of Rhydderch. Here's to the night wood. Dear werewolf, half a week from the full moon howling at the front door. Dog's tails communicate their emotional state.

Cognitive Unconscious 1

Upon opening a large charm, for a large woman, I spied a miniature living room. The sofa measured in millimetres; the house itself was maybe centimetres. I speak as I create in grayscale. The charm was sterling, I knew, not gold, not platinum. Please trust me, I'm telling you stories.

Once upon a time, I went up the lookout tower of Cardiff castle. Curled up like a kitten on the old stone roof, I couldn't come down. The staircase was spinning. The stones were blurring. I couldn't hold tight enough to the railing. Here were the steps in my first apartment that my kitten fell down on her face. The steps were too small, too narrow, too steep. Were these stairs were a phallic symbol? They measured taller than wide, of course. How many deaths in medieval times were due to falling down the stone staircases?

The house charm only comes in eighteen karat gold. There wasn't even a carrot in that kitchen. Natural carrots are yellow white. The colour of tarnished white gold in fact. Carrot flowers Queen Anne's Lace. What fish is the colour of tarnished sterling silver? I can not cook this pain anyway. If art, then fact. Trust me, I'm telling you stories.

Julia Rose Lewis

Phenomenology of the Feral IX

He had me at Chinese frying pan, really, alone I sleep like a prized fish. Comma mark on the dog bed, paused nose towards my owner's bedroom. Not in the fireplace, but the hearth is the meeting tree retold with wagging tails. The moral of the fourth branch is that curses can be reversed with tricks, so why is a woman with a horse sexual and a woman with a dog not?

Oryctolagus Cuniculus

*Bit, bite, brussels sprouts he forked and
fed me, "rabbit food" my first love said.*

"Vegetable is not a botanically useful term. Trust me,
I'm telling you stories."

These bunnies
have a well developed dewlap-
a flap
of skin
under their (mothers') chins
is used to keep offspring warm.

The warm spring of 2008,
introductory biology, inorganic chemistry, and philosophy of science where I
met the rabbit with pure white coat with pink eyes.

"I've done laboratory research on the organization and development of the nervous systems of crayfish, rabbits, leeches, and, most extensively, frogs, where the work focused on the nature of spatial representations, and the origins, organization, regulation, and significance of unpredictability in neuronal function and behaviour."

– Paul Grobstein, Eleanor A. Bliss professor of biology at Bryn Mawr College

Mother of all rabbits,
        I stand on the shoulders of a flemish giant.

Julia Rose Lewis

Phenomenology of the Feral X

We had dog breath, a broom, a dustpan, a large and unfamiliar towel all green with which to clean. The grey clothes we both wore. He worried about his coat roaning out to pewter, to the stainless steel key I keep to the apartment. Towards silver I wanted to tell him nine days and a grey-blue dog-bed ago. All those sterling eternity hoops keep him from biting my ears, white against white, I still want to bite his ears.

Phenomenology of the Feral XI

Lleu by leaf by life
leaking, fallen in ceiling
light house keep to clean

Julia Rose Lewis

Phenomenology of the Feral XII

I hold the colour of the Gwynedd sky in my head. To sleep with the ghost of his covertly large paws, typos, scent, so much depends upon the feet and math. The magician king has greater powers than his nephew; therefore, the wolves are made human only to be made into dear. The boar's neck bristles attract me. The moon waxes full this week, and we find ourselves a little feral.

Phenomenology of the Feral XIII

metaphor of were
wolves tamed to I lick when he
noses me on the hearth

Julia Rose Lewis

Phenomenology of the Feral XIV

Man's best friend takes the form add a geode (add damn the river Dee, the water falling at ease). No more of the ceiling falls on them in the later morning. Woman's best friend is a Rottweiler dreaming of sexual positions to satisfy their metaphor. It is in the nature of good dogs to sleep on the hearth; their tails close.

Cognitive Unconscious 2

Abracadabra translates to I create as I speak. Looking deeper into the house charm, my world, drained of colour. I was seeking the kitchen. The house was coming nearer and farther off as though I was using a loupe. The colour receded as the house approached, but my hands held only the house. This is known as Alice in Wonderland syndrome. It occurs as migraine surges, white caps on the brain. But I was definitely asleep. The roof of the house flipped up lightship-basket-like. Trust me, I'm telling you stories. I was peering into the house from the top bringing up my old fear of heights.

The shiny, tin-white floor of the house was rushing towards me. The house was growing again. Larger and closer. Larger and clearer. I slipped through the loupe, electron-like. Closer and clearer. The house moved forward. The opening in the roof grew to swallow my face. Trust me, I'm telling you stories. Face first and then I was inside the silver-white kitchen. I was starving. I thought I should shrink to the size of this house, this sink, and this bed. So the grey lady says, trust me, I'm telling you stories.

If Paul Grobstein was the white rabbit and I am silver, then what does this dream mean? In the silver kitchen, there should be a silver scaled fish, natural carrots, eggs, butter, onions and never Yukon gold potatoes. I am just inside the little grey lady in the sea. Trust me, I'm telling you stories.

Julia Rose Lewis

Gilfaethwy

The pirate is part magician and part thief. With all the gauze and white tape, I know the left side of his face better than the right side. Pirates, like werewolves, live tied to the moon. The dark break in the white plaster is the negative of the full moon rising.

here Gilfaethwy
gills of the fish faith you and
me these pirates see

His lupine history lingers as the silver in his beard. Wolves and domestic dogs alike contract Lyme Disease. A study in the Czech Republic, found wild boar in forest regions infected with the bacteria as well. Tell me who steals the otherworldly pigs, without magic? There is magic in the phenomenology of the feral sentenced to three years in the forest. The deer with white tails like lighthouses are host to the black-legged ticks who are host to the Borrelia burgdorferi. Lighthouses, cyclops, and lakes oh dear.

When in Doubt, Throw Grobstein on the Table

December 2008

I found some toads on the farm in the shade of the boxes filled with fake flowers to scare the horses. The toads scared the horses more, movement is sharper in black and white. Some were crushed to death when the horses shopped dirty and toppled the jumps. Charlie was the first toad I rescued who

turned into a Charlotte
was gravid and was released
nearby a river.

This was fair play for toads.

September 2009

I saw some toads in the wash stall, looking for a bath in moist stone and concrete enclosure. We say that we bathe horses, but with a hose, it more closely resembles a shower. We shower together when the water pressure is good.

Prozac code-named Zach
mascot of the slippery
brain sodality

he was not ever
slippery but leaping all
about the table

never to leave he
was ever the perfect pet
he stopped peeing me

he chased flies crickets
on computer screen and we
flipped him upside down

he let us perch him
on model horses on a
gentle rat also

Interpretative fallacy: what is sex a metaphor for?

Julia Rose Lewis

November 2009

I wonder sometimes, what did he do to make himself so big? He who was so anxious.

Mack the Big Mac sized
the terrified defensive
or depressed captive

My horse was on daily dewormer pellets and empty Strongid C buckets piled up in my living room. These were the green plastic buckets I used for storing and transporting the toads to their new home. The sides too steep and slippery there was no need for a lid or fear of carbon dioxide build up inside. They always survived my driving.

March 21st 1946 – June 28th 2011

I braked for some toads (not goats) who hoped the driveway at night.

Chipotle also
Chip for tortillas salsa
cheese burritos

be good depression
food light-headed lingerer
he dried up, and died

Paul Grobstein was the man who taught me how to tell the difference between a frog and a toad. Toads have a parotid gland, most frogs do not have this third bump behind the ears behind the eyes. Frogs will not pee on you when you kiss them. Toads are cuter, more mammalian.

Maid of Refrigerators

In the beginning,
was a big white doily-like
thing/dress. We held hands.

Brush to London poetry
of corn yellow and
off-white, the black dress I wear.
Watch something wilder
than Iowa; I tell her
the story of the
abstract refrigerator.

Bride, maid of honour:
bliss is she will wear the blush
not white dress and I
the blue. To dust the black shiny
bits of their kitchen.
The found refrigerator
is her reflection.

Julia Rose Lewis

Merely
all poems are love poems[7]

I flower you.
I wove through two.
I whatever our tattoo says you.

Good night, sleep tight, do not let anything bite us. She is made of grapes, and I am made of corn. Her breasts like champagne truffle cupcakes specify the body of the problem as a recipe. The vanilla cupcake and buttercream frosting profile her breast. The truffle on top gives the colour her nipple. She does not miss my breasts, but my butt like muffins because my breasts are not tattooed. Matching tattoos are the kiss of death if sex not friendship in love. I had always hated weddings, but I love her and Rye so I go. In a bridesmaid dress, my butt is not like corn muffins, northern, of course specify the body of the problem as a recipe. I am going to her wedding as the maid of refrigerators and feral, where she is gentle and beautiful. My tattoo might show beneath the dress. This is how we deal.

Breathing Underwater

Breathing Underwater I
after Hiatus Kaiyote

the words hates the words
hates the words hates the words hates
in water in what

Julia Rose Lewis

Breathing Underwater II

The skin thinks. Slippery the skin and briar lie the brain. Beak equidistant from each of its tentacles because it is easier to imagine than a mouth at the centre of its arms. Than a moment in a man's arms. I see you as an octopus, only, turned upside down. Head to chest to hydrocodone-cephalopod hybrid makes me want to wash my hair. If and only if how are you means tell me you are here. Dear laboratory partner for invertebrate zoology where are you means I want you beside me. Octopoda cradle.

Breathing Underwater III

Should an octopus be encouraged to juice an orange? Please sing sure. Play, sure. Like getting a flying lead change off a green horse, give to it with your inside hand. Can octopuses lip read?

If one gives an octopus enough oranges, sooner or later it will surely press the orange juice out of curiosity. The problem is not the dilution; the ocean doesn't want orange juice. Read what is left of the fruit right down to the bitter rind. The orange does not want salting, the microorganisms that live in the sea do not want for blue or green.

I am afraid of an octopus fractal, as if falling off a horse.

Julia Rose Lewis

Breathing Underwater IV

Always the shape of tear drops, behold brussels sprouts the size of eggs. From the head to the hand, dear cephalopod, suction at a distance. Octopuses do not turn green usually. Eyes a shade darker than sautéed cabbage with shallots and loads of butter derivative of a cow. Do octopuses ever fantasize about fur? Let the eggs be all of the eyes and make the omelet you bragged about. Happiness is a potato. Not seen: octopus holding a potato, because depression is a brussels sprout or the eye of the potato? This homology of food groups is all wrong. Turn up some suction cups please.

Breathing Underwater V

hemocyanin
turning blue with oxygen
copper jewellery

Julia Rose Lewis

Admiration of Hermit Crabs

You pray to the blue light house,
be alive, be lingering, dear beleaguered.

Trying to kiss under the cold waves
is the blue of distance.

Belong, here I am the hermit in the glass shell
at home with blue time.

The seat of the soul, the pineal gland, is thought
the seat of sleep. The light

of electronics turns the longing blue and
brings the loss of sleep.

As I pray to the blue light house,
you are the hermit creature in the glass shell.

Breathing Underwater VI

octopuses turn
pirates boarding fishing boats
breaking holds to feast

Julia Rose Lewis

Breathing Underwater VII

oranges are not
the only fruit formalin
preserves see creatures

Breathing Underwater VIII

Eight pieces of candied orange peel held together with an orange hard candy and more sugar. Skim and foam just of the shore, skimming forms the marmalade, the foam off the latte. Skin of the orange you think? Sugar clings to the skin. Sugar sticks to the tongue. Boiling brings us to the desired concentration of sugar. Before thermometers, there were bowls of cold water, balls, and threads for the fresh water test. Thread stage turns to soft-ball stage turns to firm-ball stage turns to hard-ball stage turns to soft crack stage turns to hard crack stage. Things I have done in the name of depression: read philosophy of science. See Grobstein's crack in the story of science as a story. Then comes the caramel realizing, clear-liquid stage heats to brown liquid stage heats to bitter and burnt. Baking takes chemistry; but cooking is a feeling for the ingredients. See the octet of cracks, yet octopuses are the opposite of brittle you must remember. Things I have done in the name of depression: make a dozen jars of crystallized ginger syrup while the lion stood guard at the door. The mother of the bean tells me about how ginger grows everywhere back home, see sheep number two please. A syrup is formed by dissolving sugar into water or milk. Octopuses are raised by their mothers. Blistering and scarring and kissing happen to the skin. Blown glass octopus are, so blown sugar octopus ought to be boiling, as with breathing underwater, brings bubbles to the surface. For now, to fill a mouth full of gingerbread fudge cupcake. Things I have done in the name of depression: become one with my bed. The orange lifesavers are turned into edible stained glass windows of a gingerbread house.

Julia Rose Lewis

Breathing Underwater IX

her in water in
water in water in what
here in water the

Breathing Underwater X

Material slowly unwinds as I leave the feathers of seagulls behind for your love, for your lover to find. Your limbs double as hands warm hands wrapped in blue linen line endings. *Vis a vis* thinking about failing and not hearing the echo the leaves are falling. To try to feel to feeler and feel here for your lover to find. Sun over wild and arid as stone says the chthonic one. Be breathing underwater. Bring again underwater breathing. Breath evenly underwater for your love. From ten tears, to seven years for your lover to find. Anterior or posterior aorta, please tattoo the artery with acute artistry. For the love of hiraeth on the inside of my foot, this cephalopod is to be read from the inside. Breath into water, merely the squid's anatomy can be compared easily. The word rests on its systemic heart, breath here. The squid sees the upside down octopus as a Rottweiler, breath here underwater. The octopus regards the upside down squid as an English teacher, together they are a pair of feet to find. A paradigm for your lover to find. I could call your demons aside, soaking them in camomile is warming and moisturizing. Pleasure, it melts into the yellow leather like hydrocodone melting down your face. Yell out for your love. Please be breathing underwater for your lover to find.

Julia Rose Lewis

Breathing Underwater XI

talking skin yellow
orange red brown-black
iridophores yes

Breathing Underwater XII

Because it is very important that there is this dash to the den to hide inside, after time and tide. Whine ruby octopus, dear red. Here is the rub: head to your broad stomach. Corundum, like octopuses and lifesavers, comes in all colours. Often mistaken for a young Enteroctopus dofleini. There is a soft test, dear octopus rubescens, your three papillae below the eyes, so very eyelash-like allow for differentiation. Tell me when I can kiss you again? With a dark red sense of humour, oh how your tentacles curl into musical notes and such. The house goes darker with age and dirt. The barnacles change their sexes. The ship is lost to sight, and the octopus is safer because the old bottle gives succour. People who love in glass bottles and all. Let there be anemones holding onto the home that is still half litter, half recycling. Not ever plastic bottles, always glass, always burnt sugar brittle and brown. Do not say fat innkeeper worm aloud, one art, one loss who I miss every day. We go to ground.

Breathing Underwater XIII

Ensis directus
intertidal bay razor
is salted from sand

Breathing Underwater XIV

You heart me, and I open up a razor clam for you. Do you see it? Octopuses have three hearts. Two branchial hearts to pump the blood to the two gills. One systemic heart to pump the body of the blood, from the heart to the stomach. Clams or snails? The fried stomachs of clams make summer with buttermilk and flour, the flavour of the digestive tract. Clam strips could be clam bellies, could be soft-shells, shape not species defines the dish. Chew it slowly. Think of a place molasses dark and safe. Adagio is a paradigm for building a ship in a bottle.

Julia Rose Lewis

Breathing Underwater XV

Notes towards an epistemology of octopuses, yes, plural. First is the way in which fantasizing about an octopus might be anything but lesbian. Remember that octopuses are mistresses of escape. From green on green to grey against grey, I liked the taste of seaweed gin, but the bottle was clear. To catch an octopus, put out the darkest glass bottle you can find. I find myself trying to catch your eye. Let us hold heads. How many heads of lettuce could an octopus carry and still travel? Tentacles out, let us count. Last, in the lee of the harbour, try to see the eel grass and cross your eyes instead.

Emissary

The alien tells you to
never trust ale from a
god-fearing people,
or a star fleet
commander
who has one of your
relatives
in jail. The red uniform
commands the red mist
that descends when one
you don't want to hug
forces you to hug.

What is an antonym for
anger? Locutus of Borg
or
the round bitterness
could
break apart like an egg
shell.

"Malevolent, aggressive,
adversarial," declares
the alien holding the
baseball bat. Meaning
you will explain
baseball to non-
corporeal lifeforms,
"Benjamin, my mate,
kisses on the cheek,
and he finds me
anything, where's the
hardship in that?

This explains kissing to
non-corporeal life-
forms. Inside the blue-
white light of the
wormhole, who created
an impossible
planet, who will mature
into guerrilla knitting?
The Kai,
the alien spiritual leader,
keeps grabbing at your
earlobes to feel your
soul, it will mature
into trees & various
plant life.

Julia Rose Lewis

Opaka calls the
wormhole the celestial
temple.

The Cardassians want to
possess
the wormhole. You
move your home to the
mouth of the wormhole,
it is not linear to need a
brain, half a pear, a tear
of the prophet, and forty
feet.[8]

Breathing Underwater XVI

Could us octopuses play a game of string figures together? From the string to the tentacle bridge thing from the tentacle to the string again. The thinking beak has another trick: breathing above water. Genius of an odd kind indeed. Gripping equals thinking would you say so model organism? The human paradigm thinks of the mantle. Lie close to the suction cups, so think arms think without a somatotopic map. Genus octopus stores their nerve cords in their tentacles. Tentacles upon tentacles, these thinking cups possess chemical sensors to keep from sticking to self. Dear octopus, tentacles up today? What do you have on today means what plots are you threading for today. Tentacles do not tangle but string can knot. What about knitting? Here goes a figure of sixteen. Definition of chthonic: see fantasy of lying on the sea floor, before, on my back, my head to your stomach still. And so we come full circle, bubble full of air, to breathing underwater.

Summer of Gummy Bears

Lingering Question

When life hands you lemon flavoured gummy bears, then drive. The dancing bear turned into the gold bear turned into the gummy bear. The illusion of travel, the illusion of being a turtle in a Walmart parking lot, the stereotyped behaviour of animals in the zoo. The pineapple flavoured gummy bears are clearer, sometimes, the grape flavour is colourless. This sweet and squeezable candy can be organic and/or vegan when the gelatine is replaced with pectin. What hallucination makes lemons taste yellower than pineapples?

ha you sign gnash un-
less *ananas ne parlent pas*
plus airplanes bear fruit

Julia Rose Lewis

I Bring You Bears and Raspberries

only beet juice blood
not ethidium bromide
pink-red dye cast bears

Anatomy of a red gummy bear, if you think mashed raspberries resemble blood, then you have never seen blood, mammalian blood. Nantucket red is the converse of hunting pinks. Blood is neither magenta nor blue, it is brown as the water from the well at Hibid Farm. The old bottom of the old gate was scalpel sharp aluminium, I think. The iron-rich water we used to wash down the wash stall after the obsidian pony cut open her femoral artery. It was red pear liquid everywhere and covering everyone standing there. She did not die, but oh my blood!

The Greening of the Bears

hay and strawberries
someday, the stems, the hairy
leaves gummy bears green

Not the red of beets or cranberries for these candies; anatomy of a strawberry gummy bear is liquid tsavorite garnets for organs. Gummy bears and arabinose and ribose were all named for gum arabic, resin from the acacia tree. Safer to extract the deoxyribonucleic acid from strawberries than make gummy bears at home. The body of the problem is glucose. My sister gave me a recipe for preparing strawberry DNA; her ingredients are frozen strawberries, shampoo, table salt, ethanol or isopropanol. All the required equipment can be found in the kitchen: coffee-filter, funnel, sealable sandwich bags. Like dissolves like when the whitish strands of DNA are extracted from strawberries, the liquid left behind is red.

Julia Rose Lewis

Ginger Bears with the Wifey

fire, corn, fire, foyer,
fire, corn, fire, fruit, corn, fire, foyer,
fire, corn, fire, foyer

Of food and fire-pit, I peel and de-caterpillar the corn for the wifey. We are celebrating our eleventh anniversary with corn and steel coloured wool. She makes me cry with wasabi; she makes me cry with laughter. In honour of the painting we call big ass bun buns and fruit. Always replace the word vegetable with festival; it is more knowable than *ananas banane orangensaft*.

Is ginger root a festival? She knows the week to buy me crystallized ginger root that has been dipped in dark chocolate. We reimagine the orange gummy bear as ginger root instead of fruit.

When she asks me how it feels to come out of the ginger paper bag, I reply that first is first and second is second with respect to the roundabouts. Do you think they are going to come over and ask us to stop saying corn and fire?

The Quaker Kind

If there were a blueberry gummy bear, it would be the colour of the teeshirt she loved, part mother, partner in crime. Unconditional love is a human construct like blueberry leather clogs. There is something of the glass essay about us. Acid loving bilberry plants are grown with manure compost on New Jersey farms. Unconditional love is a human construct like a farm built one stall at a time. I was always about to fall in love with the mare with a blueberry gummy bear in her eye.

sour currant and sweet
blueberry pairs of gummy
bears are holding hands

Julia Rose Lewis

'This is Vintage Julia'

shit, Diet Pepsi
junior year pre-road kill, breast
cancer, chemistry

Remember: she prefers violet syrup, and I prefer violet extract. If gelatine is used in place of agar or pectin, a beef flavour may contaminate the gummy bears. Neither black carrot juice nor grape juice concentrate may be able to cover up the beef flavour of the gelatine. I am her grape, and she is my violet gummy bear. She loves the intrigue of the painting of white eggplant surrounded by three apples. The wind loves her breasts so she is a dangerous curve. She does not back down up the hill, ever, we walk about in tropical storms and hurricanes. Forever, we would prefer to share the beach with the wind and sand and rain in place, instead of man people. We have devolved into affirmative sheep amongst the Jeep Wranglers.

Cherries to Old Nantucket

Begin with a cube of sugar in an old fashioned glass, due to the humidity all sugar here is more or less regular cubes. Hint, hint, nudge, nudge, insert holding pattern here. Muddle the sugar with bitters as with lightship baskets woven in a month's duty of boredom. As with gummy bears, recipes disagree on the relative amounts of plain water and flavouring bitters. The oval purses, otherwise known as friendship baskets are traditionally eight inches in size large enough to hold a man's head. Add ice cubes and rye whiskey to the glass. I hold this bulk in the corner of my elbow, this old lightship basket, house sing a stolen head. Garnish the drink with an orange or lemon twist. Is a maraschino cherry, so much more cheery than a cherry gummy bear?

finish with the fog
rolling toward the wood deck and
late reservation

Julia Rose Lewis

Sand Woman, Sour Woman

granny smith apple
blown sugar green glass apple
blowing glass essay

Sweeping a carpet, like cleaning out a stall, everyday with broom and shovel and plastic pitchfork, the paddocks too. Unconditional love is not natural and it is not what animals offer us; her horse is part magpie with bowling pin ears and four white hooves. Sour apple, sour grapes, we sit on her mother's uneven stone steps being aware our failures, we are all women here because mares are cheaper than geldings. Sour apple, sour cherries, still blond, I hate her hair, I loved it so when it was auburn, my colour, it was dyed then too, I was just young enough not to know. What the sour orange! the sour gummy bear flavours are the same as the sweet. They are covered with sour sand. This was the summer that everyone told me to make peace with my mother before she died. And I did, sort of, sew our failures together.

Hair of the Gummy Bear

the star ruby ring
like a cranberry caught out
of falling sunlight

The cranberry festival not vegetables comes. He gives us fried green tomatoes; he is a bold thing to us Bostonians. We name our friend hair, because of the unbearable beauty of his hair. Anatomy of the heart turned upside down is an onion. Something natural, I touched hair's hair because a bit of tree flake, miss and bark and mould fell into it, and he hugged me. The origin of the notion that the onion turned upside down is a heart. The wifey and the momsie go to him for lobster rolls; this is something natural. Listen to the leaves of the trees moving, was it lichen instead of moss? We miss him opposite of provisions, if he leaves this faraway land, will he live longer? Once upon a time, my wife and I fell in love with the same man; the mother of all gummy bears for she and I to share.

Julia Rose Lewis

Happy Stroll

hair of the rabbit
is blond, is blending into
lightship basket wood

The wood of pines is used for the staves. Anatomy of a lightship basket: the moulds were made from old, cut up ships' masts. The skull of an adult human has the volume to hold a juvenile rabbit. Teachers weave with their students lightships baskets to fill with their reflections. The base, stave, weaver, inner rim, outer rim, top cane, cross lashing, handle and bail, button, wooden ear, plug. Under the rabbit's ears lie bone and from brain. The button and plug of lightship baskets may be made from either ebony or whale ivory. I bought a human brain jello mould on sale after halloween, because I came from the Grobstein laboratory. Try to imagine the smell of formaldehyde, hint orange liqueur. I mixed white chocolate with peppermint, black food colouring and poured into the mould for my white rabbit. Once a upon a time, this was the anatomy of Christmas.

Notes

[1] http://www.brynmawr.edu/chemistry/swhite.html

[2] Lerner, Alan Jay, 'I Could Have Danced All Night' in *My Fair Lady: Vocal Score* (Faber Music Ltd: London, 1999), pp. 22-37.

[3] Shakespeare, William, *The Tempest* (OUP: Oxford, 2008), Act V, ll.1-5.

[4] Fowler, S. J., *The Rottweiler's Guide to the Dog Owner* (Eyewear Publishing: London, 2014).

[5] Lewis, Gwyneth, *The Meat Tree :New Stories from the Mabinogion* (Seren: Bridgend, 2013)

[6] Grantz, Jeffrey, *The Mabinogion* (Penguin: London, 1976).

[7] line taken from the James Galvin poem, 'Blue or Green'

[8] This poem makes extensive use of lines from the collaborative poetry collection *Forty Feet* by David Berridge and S.J. Fowler as well as the Star Trek Deep Space Nine Pilot episode, *Emissary*.

Berridge, D., & Fowler, S. J., *Forty Feet* (Knives Forks and Spoons: Newton-le-Willows, 2016). *Star Trek: Deep Space Nine, Emissary.* Dir. David Carson. Paramount Television. 1995.

www.ingramcontent.com/pod-product-compliance
Lightning Source LLC
Chambersburg PA
CBHW050455110426
42743CB00017B/3377